A

Greater Migration

By: Robert M. Walker

ISBN 978 0 578 11550 4

Dedicated To:

A Revolutionary's Heart

Acknowledgements

Utmost honor and praise to my Lord and Savior Jesus Christ. This book is a testament to YOUR word in 2 Corinthians 12:9. I have come to understand the love, strength, and power of YOUR Grace. My recognition of YOUR Grace in my life has empowered me to walk with a blessed assurance. Any glory this book receives is YOURS, not mine. It was YOUR strength through me that put these words on paper. I am merely a vessel chosen by YOU. Thank YOU for choosing me.

To my mother, without your revolution, my revolution would not be possible. Thank you for all the love you showed me as a child. Your love taught me self-worth. Thank you for sacrificing to provide an education and not gym shoes, clothes, or game systems. Your sacrifice taught me priorities. Thank you for your relentless discipline of me as a child. Your discipline taught me there are consequences for my actions. Subsequently, at the age of thirteen I changed my behavior and attitude. Realizing I was not willing to pay those consequences that were sure to come if I continued to fight and misbehave.

To John, my self-appointed surrogate father. Turning eighteen and graduating high school marked a great transition for me. A transition different from what all young adults go through during that period. I decided the hurt of my absent father would no longer walk with me. I was eighteen and did not need my father, or any father, ever again. I am happy that GOD knew I would need a father more than ever after the age of eighteen. HE sent you to be that father for me. It is hard to explain the dedication and love you have for me to others. The best blessings are often unexplainable. The timeliness of your presence in my life is not lost upon me. At times you were the only parent I communicated or had a relationship with. I would not have made it to my eighteenth birthday without my mother. I would not have made it to my twenty-seventh birthday without my father. Thank you.

Corey I am truly appreciative of how close we have grown as brothers in our adult years. Your love and support has kept me going at times when I was ready to throw in the towel. I am extremely proud and inspired by the husband and father you are to your family. I only hope to one day be the same. I love you.

B-ball, Jason, Hasri, Ilya, and Kareem I could not ask for better friends. I never thought I would be able to replace the closeness I shared with my childhood friends. However, in our friendships I have recaptured that childhood camaraderie.

Chastity our relationship is very special to me. The wisdom and support you have given me is irreplaceable. Our conversations are always profound and comforting. I focus on the game and not pay attention to the score.

To the Walker family and my childhood friends all the great times we shared growing up inspired this book. Those memories I could never forget. That is why I cannot run a way from you all, the West Side of Chicago, or the African American community. THANK YOU.

Ω

"In my heart, I have to believe that there is hope for the underdog. Everyday I awaken, I want to stand beside the man who is not expected to win"

Foreword

Black bodies in motion have always caused a profound impact in our world. Economic gain or social transformations are the two common effects from their movement. Black bodies were the first great commodities of the global economy. The Black bodies in the Middle Passage were the foundation for great economic strides in the New World. The free labor stolen from those Black bodies built the wealth of our nation. The greatest threat to our Union was the ascension of the Black body from slave to free man. America would live out its ideals or perish under hypocrisy. Contemporary Black bodies yield even more economic benefits through motion. The introduction of the Black body has created billion dollar industries. Professional athletics, music entertainment, and the prison system generate billions in profits from the running, jumping, performing, and cheap labor of Black bodies. Black bodies marched America into its greatest social reform. The Civil Rights Movement resonates throughout the world. That movement of Black bodies in the 1960's has been the inspiration for social equality both domestically and abroad. The sword of justice crafted from the Civil Rights Movement has won the rights of many marginalized groups.

Black bodies in motion have inspired this world in powerful ways. Through sports, entertainment or activism Black bodies have sparked change in our world.

This book seeks to ignite another movement of Black bodies. The creation of thriving mixed-income African American neighborhoods is the goal. The book is a rallying cry to privileged African Americans. All of our privileged are being called upon, first generation and those who inherited it from their parents or grandparents. In our privilege are the tools needed to recapture the African American community from the current oppressive forces that grip it. The success of this movement will echo beyond the African American community. The gap between rich and poor has drastically widened. Social mobility is disappearing. America is at a critical adjustment period. It can restructure around creating a stable and growing middle class, or focus on the top half, while the bottom half increases and is left stranded. Privileged African Americans must take the front lines of this battle. Our people comprise the majority of those being left behind. We must craft a new sword of justice. This sword will protect the poor against economic, political, and educational abandonment. Eliminating the physical separation between rich and poor is the starting point. We must become neighbors again and realign our interest. The return of privileged African Americans to live in poor African American neighborhoods is key. Our community's success will be the blueprint for securing the rights of all poor people in America.

Introduction

In life we interact, spend extended periods of time within, join and become a part of communities other than those we are born into. I have become a part of and interacted with many communities outside of the African American community. My first experience with a community other than my African American community was in the sixth grade when I travelled to Huntsville, Alabama for Space Camp. Two other public school students and I won the trip through a writing competition. This would be my first time in an environment that was not majority underprivileged African Americans. Next I left Chicago for a high school basketball camp in Georgetown, Kentucky. I roomed with a Caucasian tobacco chewing Floridian who graciously lent me one of his covers because I was unaware that one would not be provided. For my college years I entered into a majority Caucasian world of great prestige, privilege and wealth. My four years a part of this community would shape my dedication to the African American community more than any other experience in my life. One summer break during undergraduate I lived in Cape Town, South Africa for ten weeks. For the first time in my life I interacted with a community that was poorer than my own. Nothing inspired me more than the hope within the townships of Cape Town despite the extreme poverty. I spent three weeks in Addis Ababa, Ethiopia the summer before starting law school. It made me both proud and envious of the great history of this African nation, having never been colonized, their history spanning back to BC, and their ancient castles. I took a European trip the summer after my first year of law school visiting: Barcelona, Spain; Paris, France; Rome and Florence, Italy. Most recently I travelled to Fiji and New Zealand as a part of an International Travel Project for law school.

An essential component of life's journey is interacting and learning from other communities. The exchanging of cultures develops an understanding that enables us to live together and appreciate the uniqueness in all communities. Through communing we learn ways to improve our community or better other communities. This book is not a call for segregating or stopping the fellowship between African Americans and other communities. This book is not focused on those temporary periods away from the African American community for growth and beneficial life experience. This book is about the pervasive physical, social, economic, and political abandonment of the African American community by privileged

African Americans. A migration took place after desegregation. The opportunity to live among America's elite propelled many privileged African Americans to separate themselves from the problems within our community.

With desegregation America could not continue denying privileged African Americans a seat amongst its elite. The defeat of Jim Crow meant that America now had to recognize African American achievement as its own. Without segregation a greater number of African Americans were able to achieve more pedagogical, professional, and financial success. The number of African American millionaires, college graduates, and professionals increased. Our community has had a privileged class dating back to the Reconstruction period. We had our doctors, lawyers, politicians, scholars, athletes, millionaires and other professionals before desegregation. However, the era of privilege following desegregation was different. During segregation privileged African Americans were rejected by America along with the rest of our community. No matter how educated or accomplished, an African American was treated as a second-class citizen.

America's racism confined privileged African Americans within our community. Privileged African Americans could

only get their recognition, support, and enjoy their
success within our community. The result of this racial
containment was the emergence of neighborhoods like
Greenwood in Tulsa, Oklahoma. This neighborhood was known
as the " The Negro Wall Street." Thriving African American
neighborhoods like Greenwood were created because
segregation left our people with the only option of
standing together, privileged and unprivileged.
Desegregation brought the disappearance of thriving African
American neighborhoods. Our privileged fled for that
American elitism that had been denied them since
Reconstruction.

Desegregation was followed by a period of new
oppression and resistance to African American progress. No
longer could America legally keep African Americans
separated and inferior to its other citizens. But, America
was not ready to see too many of us ascend into its upper
class. America would make the African American community
its de facto underclass. Conditions were put in place after
the Civil Rights Movement that stunted the growth of our
community following that great victory through struggle.
The FBI COINTELPRO program and the introduction of drugs
into the African American community effectively neutralized
Black revolutionary thought and action. Federal and local

law enforcement agencies targeted African American leaders, from Dr. King to the Black Panthers, as if they were criminals. Most of our leaders were assassinated or falsely imprisoned to stop their influence within our community. The drug culture was implanted into the African American community as the culture of intellectualism, progressivism, and revolutionary action was stomped out.

The government created drug culture, combined with the flight of our privileged, has placed the African American community in a cycle of oppression. Today African American primary and secondary public school students attend homogenous schools inferior in quality of instruction, resources, and infrastructure than homogenous publics schools of their Caucasian counterparts. Brown v. Board of Education has effectively been erased. The lack of quality education is attributed to the violent, drug-ridden neighborhoods African American students live and attend school within. Property values are a crucial determinant of public school funding. The violence from the drug culture keeps property values down in our neighborhoods. Without quality education African American youth are left with few options to provide a livelihood for themselves. Faced with the choice between a minimum wage job and earning fast money selling drugs, it is no surprise that many choose the latter.

Economic exploitation is another major component of this oppressive cycle. An overwhelming majority of the business owners in African American neighborhoods reside outside our neighborhoods. Operation costs are higher in our neighborhoods because of the violence. Business owners alleviate the higher operation costs by selling poor quality products and services at marked-up prices. The violence scares better businesses away, so there are no alternatives. These exploitative owners operate with impunity. These owners are not invested in our community. Their sole objective is to profit from the oppressive conditions. They sell their knockoff, expired products in our neighborhoods behind bulletproof glass. At night you must make your purchase through a window because they won't allow us into their store. They sell cigarettes and alcohol to our underage children. These owners want to profit from African American neighborhoods so long as they do not have to touch or be touched by the chaos that exist there.

The African American community, although very poor individually, collectively are a consumer force. Our spending power does not benefit our community. The many dollars we spend leave our community never to return. These business owners do not reinvest in our neighborhoods. Residents of our neighborhoods are usually not employed by these businesses. The quality of life within our neighborhoods is not improved by these businesses. Why would they? They make a great profit exploiting the conditions. Economic exploitation outsources the benefits of our community's consumer power to better other communities.

Our community has been in a state of emergency for decades. The oppressive forces that have been present throughout our history in this country have been reworked. An implicit form of oppression replaced segregation. The effect is the same, the creation of a second-class African American citizenry. African American male high school students have a fifty percent dropout rate. One out of three African American males will be incarcerated during their lifetime. The recidivism rate is eight-five percent amongst African American males. Teenage pregnancy is highest amongst our young woman. Most African American children are raised in single-mother households. Struggling African Americans cannot fully participate in our American democracy. Their preoccupation with surviving leaves little room for politics.

Our community's issues are not at the forefront of our nation's agenda. "Sexting" and texting while driving are of greater concern. Improving the state of the African American community is behind these "epidemics" on our country's social agenda. Even our first African American President will not directly address issues particular to our community. He emphatically stated that he would not pursue policy particular to improving the African American plight. But, he has no problem enacting legislation for immigration issues and speaking out for Gay rights.

Today's African American privileged must reinsert ourselves and take up the fight for our community. There needs to be a migration of us returning to live in poor African American neighborhoods. Privileged includes all African Americans that have attained the resources to live outside and separate from poor African American neighborhoods. Our physical presence is paramount to changing the conditions in our neighborhoods. Our physical presence will be the start of the reemergence of our community's powerful revolutionary voice. The one that song us through slavery, and marched us to our civil rights. Our return will be the beginning of the next evolution in our struggle for equality in this country.

Our Ghetto University

The African American community's value goes
unrecognized by our country. The extreme violence and
underachievement presumably makes our neighborhoods
worthless. This is why America has abandoned them.
Admittedly, African Americans as well do not recognize the
value of our own community. We often characterize our
success as escaping the poor neighborhoods most of us grow
up in or wear it as a badge of honor to have not grown up
in an African American neighborhood, attributing our better
life to geography. There is an association of all bad
things with our community, all good things existing
outside. There is no acknowledgement of the significance
our community holds for us as a people. Our community
equips us for the battles we face in this country. Without
the lessons of faith, love, support, self-worth,
perseverance, toughness, and forgiveness we could not
survive. The strength we have needed and will need going
forward is cultivated within our community. Our survival as
a people in America is cultivated in the African American
community, nowhere else. The progression of our people is
permanently tied to the condition of our community. The

fight to improve our people starts with building a thriving African American community.

Blackness is under attack everyday in America. The attacks of today are not explicit legalized oppression, like slavery and segregation; rather contemporary American society implicitly casts our race into its bottom class. The fact that American media's depiction of us has convinced our children that Black dolls are not as pretty or virtuous as white dolls is the perfect example. Blackness has been made inherently inferior, aesthetically unpleasing, intellectually inept, evil, criminal, and to be feared. Meeting these assumptions in our daily lives places a great burden upon the shoulders of our people.

Privileged African Americans especially can testify to the weight we feel from this burden. A friend shared with me the uneasiness he feels while riding the elevator of his high-rise building in downtown Chicago. The presumptive looks of him not belonging and looks of fear from fellow Caucasian riders create his discomfort. He becomes consumed with putting them at ease about his presence. How can he alleviate his Blackness for them? Another friend expressed her anger about being constantly mistaken for an employee in retail stores despite being dressed in business clothes and not wearing a nametag. The attire for her executive

position does not overcome her Blackness. My personal
experience of walking to my law school's parking lot, and
having a Caucasian female become so unnerved that she
blurted out, "You're scaring me." My Blackness caused her
to assume that I was following her and not simply walking
to my vehicle in the same parking lot.

Faced with these daily attacks, it is easy to see how
one can become self-conscious about their Blackness, even
adopting a negative mentality. The African American
community provides the refuge where the value of Blackness
can be taught, affirmed, nurtured, and developed into
concepts that counteract America's attacks. The great faith
within our community strengthened our ancestors to endure
slavery. The radical idea of "Black is beautiful" inspired
our people to embrace and celebrate the unique aesthetic
features of our Blackness. The revolutionary cry "Black
Power" represents the force of political and social change
our community became. These foundations that have upheld
Blackness could only be born inside our community. Our
society still does not embrace Blackness as it's own.
Blackness is still viewed as separate and adversative to
American society. American society's racist psyche is still
fearful of these powerful antithetical concepts, and those
yet to be born. Our society's blindness makes it necessary

for the African American community to still be the refuge it has been in the past.

Faith is the foundation upon which any oppressed people's initial belief in change rests. The faith that strengthened our ancestors during slavery was passed down through the generations. This faith has fueled us as individuals and as a community in our victories of progress in this country. My dogged belief that education was key for overcoming the obstacles African American males born to low-income single-mothers face, was pure faith. Faith is the substance of things hoped for, the evidence of things unseen. There was no evidence that I could see in my family, friends or surroundings that substantiated my belief. I knew no lawyers, or even anyone that had attended law school. In fact, the evidence showed that athletics, entertainment or acquiescence were my only options. My ancestors had not experienced freedom in America when they first desired to possess it. The evidence supported the conclusion that freedom was for white people. **But faith.** Faith drove my ancestors to seek and sacrifice for victory over their momentary impossibility. I inherited this faith from my ancestors, and with it overcame my momentary impossibility. One of the few things our history of oppression has not robbed our people of is this inheritance of faith. This reservoir of faith lives within the African American community. Our people will always need to tap into that reservoir to battle momentary impossibilities. If we continue to allow our community to descend, our great inheritance will perish with it. Future generations will be left without our people's greatest source of strength.

"Black is beautiful" is not only an aesthetic idea. It is also the recognition of the beauty in our people's struggle in America. It taught African Americans to have pride rather than shame about our history of suffering. One could easily see weakness in our ancestors' bondage. However, the beauty lies in the power our struggle developed in us. When a community is forced to endure the most heinous conditions, does not perish, but survives and eventually obtains victory, it becomes indestructible. Slavery made the African American community indestructible. If we survived slavery as a community, there is nothing that we cannot face and defeat. This beauty in Blackness allows us to face any conditions set against us with an unwavering confidence that *We Shall Overcome.* Remembering our beauty means that we take up any battle knowing that it is already won. My personal battles with feelings of academic, social, and economic inadequacy as I journeyed from the West Side of Chicago into an elite undergraduate institution, corporate job, then top tier law school, were easily faced after reflections on the beauty in my Blackness. If I could survive the West Side of Chicago and am descendant from survivors of the middle passage, slavery, and segregation, my current battles are minor. There is no struggle you can give us that we cannot overcome. **Black is beautiful**. Our people cannot be discouraged by the state of the African American community today. We must take up this fight remembering our beauty. The battle is already won.

"Black power" is the African American community's faith and beauty put into action. It is the realization of our ability to change the circumstances and move America closer to its ideals. "Black Power" is not anti-American. "Black Power" represents the awakening of any oppressed community that seeks a just world because it has known injustice too long. "Black Power", and all that it stands for, is equivalent to our country's Declaration of Independence. Both are the realization of oppressed people that only revolutionary action will bring about the justice they seek.

> We hold these truths to be self-evident, that all men are created equal, that they are endowed by their Creator with certain unalienable Rights, that among these are Life, Liberty and the pursuit of Happiness. That to secure these rights, Governments are instituted among Men, deriving their just powers from

the consent of the governed--That whenever any Form of Government becomes destructive of these ends, it is the Right of the People to alter or to abolish it, and to institute new Government, laying its foundation on such principles and organizing its powers in such form, as to them shall seem most likely to effect their Safety and Happiness.

The state of our community today is unacceptable. America is not fully living up to its ideals, and our people suffer disproportionately. "Black Power" means that change is within our hands. Our community must again implement "Black Power" to change our community and America. We do not need anyone to do it for us. We need not be patient with America. We are Americans. Once we decide that now is the time for America to hold true to its ideals, it is our duty as Americans to do the work progress requires. This is not a new fight for the African American community. "Black Power" has won the victory of progress before. It can be won again.

The African American community is not a barrier from which we seek to escape. We must not adopt the oppressive attitude that believes our neighborhoods are the problem. As if African Americans are incapable of living with one another in thriving neighborhoods. We must appreciate the irreplaceable importance of our community: the inherited faith, our beauty, and political and social power. We must preserve it. Our community's current distressing state is the result of oppression, not an organic outcome of African Americans living together. Flight and fear of our neighborhoods exacerbate the affect of the oppressive forces.

My law school graduation will not mark my escape from my West Side of Chicago neighborhood. It will be the culmination of my striving to break those barriers placed in front of the African American community. By no means was the West Side of Chicago one of those barriers. My African American community on Chicago's West Side instilled in me the qualities that brought me success. My community taught me that despite having nothing, I was something. My ambition was born from this. My community raised me to be tough. I never quit because of this. My community taught me I am invincible. I have an unbreakable self-confidence because of this. I am one hundred percent a product of my environment. I am an example of what can be achieved from African American neighborhoods absent the obstacles. I was blessed with opportunities through which I circumvented the pitfalls that beset so many in my community. There are so many in my community with my same ability, if not more, who simply lack opportunities to succeed. This is why I cannot accept that the community or the people within it are the problem. The African American community is valuable to our people and to America. We must change its current state. Our victory will recapture tremendous amounts of lost potential that will benefit America as a whole.

School Days

My undergraduate years were paramount to my return to the West Side of Chicago to improve the conditions there. My disadvantaged background coupled with my experience attending a prestigious undergraduate institution provided perspective from both ends of the spectrum. With this perspective, I concluded resources are what most separate these two communities. A community's ability to grow and harness their resources dictates its quality of life. The few resources of my West Side of Chicago community are too often exploited, so it deteriorates. My undergraduate community possesses vast resources that are properly allocated so it flourishes. A person's community determines their future more than their drive, work ethic, or intellectual ability. The road to success from underprivileged communities is unpaved with huge chunks of the road missing and no signs to direct one's path. Privileged communities' road to success is newly paved with speed bumps, rest stops, and convenience stations along the way. Wealth too often determines the winners and losers in this country, not one's desire to succeed. Exposed to this truth, I decided my new privilege would not blind me from the reality of why many African Americans underachieve. I cannot accept wealth predetermining the fate of my people.

My undergraduate academic struggles are the perfect analogy for the overwhelming underachievement within the African American community. My zeal for learning, work ethic, determination, intellectual ability and drive matched that of my classmates. Quality of education is what separated us. I went from being the Salutatorian of my high school class to the bottom half of my undergraduate class. My high school's five thousand dollar tuition could not compete with my classmates' high schools' thirty thousand dollar tuition. Resources dictate quality of education. The gap created by the difference in quality of education is not easily erased. I utilized my professors, teacher's assistants, and tutors just to maintain my position in the bottom half. The impact of this gap can be devastating. For example, after receiving my ACT scores I wanted to know what my older brothers scored. I was shocked to learn that their scores were ten points lower then mine. Both were honor students at the Chicago Public High School they attended. I had no delusions about my intellectual ability being that much greater than their own. The correlation between a school's resources and the development of its students' natural abilities became clear. Most African

American students attend failing public schools like my brothers. Their natural abilities are not nurtured and augmented. Every year spent in these failing public schools places them further into America's bottom half. Their fates are tied to their community and school's resources, not their intelligence or desire to learn. Analogous to my undergraduate experience, their education has not adequately prepared them to compete with their peers.

My undergraduate experience presented me with a choice. It is the decision that all privileged African Americans face. Will we accept African American inferiority? Our privilege has placed us on the better side of this social construct so many find it easier to acquiesce. With assimilation comes a belief that our privilege has placed us above African Americans as well. A conversation with a fellow African American undergraduate student illustrates this best. While discussing law school and careers as attorneys this student asserted they would be able to easily defeat any African American attorney they come up against. Their syllogism was affirmative action has pushed most African Americans through under less stringent requirements. Their pedigree of graduating from a top boarding school and our undergraduate institution has required them to meet much higher standards. Therefore, they are vastly superior then any African American attorney they would ever face. They made it clear that it was not a slander, just a fact. Most privileged African Americans make similar deductions, albeit not as ugly. Fact, the Caucasian neighborhood is better than the African American neighborhood because it is safer, cleaner, and quieter. Fact, the majority Caucasian primary, middle, or secondary school is a better place for my children because it has better teachers, curriculum, extracurricular activities, and is safer. These choices give no credence to how today's conditions are the residual effects of yesterday's oppression. By choosing to now benefit from those effects, opposed to repairing our community, we condone the white supremacy of the past. Too often we privileged tolerate the inferiority of our community. We have placed all of the significance on our individual battle. Believing victory for our community is impossible.

I can never accept African American inferiority. I can never accept inferiority period. No matter the group of people it is being imposed upon. I had been prepared for my own inferiority once before in life, and resoundingly proved that theorist wrong. Before departing for Space Camp my sixth grade teacher pulled me aside after school. She informed me the students I would be interacting with at

Space Camp would be much smarter than me. My goal should be to stay out of trouble and learn from the other students. There was no need for me to try to succeed at Space Camp. I was inferior and should accept it. Returning I proudly showed my sixth grade teacher I received the only award given out at Space Camp. The two camp counselors over the respective groups bestow one award to the student who best demonstrated teamwork and leadership during their week at Space Camp. I was given this leadership medal.

Inferiority is not real. Inferiority is a weapon used to discourage an individual or group of people from seeking transformation. Inferiority, if accepted, is self-fulfilling. Inferiority when not accepted is easily disproven. My undergraduate experience was not affirmation of African American inferiority for me. I graduated with an understanding of why the difference between my home community and my undergraduate community existed. It confirmed that the conditions are not organic, but by design. My diploma was proof that the design can be changed.

My most significant change during undergraduate was the eradication of my tolerance for violence. Living in an environment without violence enlightened me. I began to recognize my desensitization to the prevalent violence of my home environment. Growing up in certain Chicago neighborhoods a person learns to accept, even expect, a high volume of violence daily. When it occurs people are not shocked or shaken by it, life continues on virtually without missing a beat. It pauses long enough to say R.I.P. Literally, my first day home after my freshman year a man was shot on the corner of my city block. My reaction to such violence was different from the past. I was no longer desensitized to it. I had spent the majority of the year in an environment where such violence is unheard. Seeing the desensitized reactions of my neighbors gave me a new perspective. The person was shot, but not killed. The paramedics and police came to pick him up. Within thirty minutes after this shooting my city block was back to normal. Children were back playing at the schoolyard on the corner. The corner became full with the people who were there before the shooting. The corner candy store was back open for business. There was no increase in police presence. There was no sign that something traumatic as a person being shot had occurred.

I realized just how tolerant everyone is of the violence on my city block, in my neighborhood, in the African American community. The residents, law enforcement, politicians, America all tolerate this violence. People are no longer shocked by this violence. It has become part and parcel of African American neighborhoods. The tolerance is reflected in the lackluster efforts to stop the violence. Chicago had more deaths in one year than American causalities in the Iraq war and there was no state of emergency declared. Local, state, and federal law enforcement did not unite to ensure any neighborhood, community, or city within this country never experiences loss of life at a rate higher than a warzone. My lack of tolerance for the violence pushed me to return. I could not tolerate this violence from afar. **We cannot change it from afar.**

My college experience birth my determination to return to the West Side of Chicago and counteract those conditions that are causing its decay. I developed a new sense of responsibility for my home community. The things I gained and learned would return with me. Applying these tools I will exact some change, if only minute. Thriving communities are built and sustained through continuous efforts for progress. The future of the African American community lies within the hands of individuals who are willing to sacrifice for progress. Those most fortunate and privileged play a significant role in community building. Privileged African Americans possess the tools needed to

spark a new age of progress in our community. This progress
starts with our return.

A Greater Migration

On July 5, 1852 Frederick Douglass was asked to address an audience in commemoration of Independence Day. Douglass, the grateful Negro, should take great joys in a celebration of independence, being an escaped slave now scholar and abolitionist. These were the assumptions of the audience he addressed. However, Douglass found nothing celebratory in his personal independence when slavery was still the reality for Negros. Douglass' privileged station and personal victory did not erase his vigilance for the Negros' plight.

Fellow citizens, pardon me, allow me to ask, why am I called upon to speak here today? What have I, or those I represent, to do with your national independence? Are the great principles of political freedom and of natural justice, embodied in that Declaration of Independence, extended to us? And am I, therefore, called upon to bring our humble offering to the national altar, and to confess the benefits and express devout gratitude for the blessings resulting from your independence to us?

But such is not the state of the case. I say it with a sad sense of the disparity between us. I am not included within the pale of glorious anniversary! Your high independence only reveals the immeasurable distance between us. The blessings in which you, this day, rejoice are not enjoyed in common. The rich inheritance of justice, liberty, prosperity and independence, bequeathed by your fathers, is shared by you, not by me. The sunlight that brought light and healing to you, has brought stripes and death to me. This Fourth July is yours, not mine. You may rejoice, I must mourn. To drag a man in fetters into the grand illuminated temple of liberty, and call upon him to join you in joyous anthems, were inhuman mockery and sacrilegious irony. Do you mean, citizens, to mock me, by asking to speak today?

Fellow citizens, above your national, tumultuous joy, I hear the mournful wail of millions! Whose chains, heavy and grievous yesterday, are, today, rendered more intolerable by the jubilee shouts that reach them. If I do forget, if I do not faithfully remember those bleeding children of sorrow this day, may my right hand forget her cunning, and may my tongue cleave to the roof of my mouth! To forget them, to pass lightly over their wrongs, and to chime in with the popular theme, would be treason most scandalous and shocking, and would make me a reproach before God and the world. My subject, then, fellow citizens, is American slavery. I shall see this day and its popular characteristics from the slave's point of view. Standing there identified with the American bondman, making his wrongs mine, I do not hesitate to declare, with all my soul, that the character and conduct of this nation never looked blacker to me than on this 4th of July! Whether we turn to the declarations of the past, or to the professions of the present, the conduct of the nation seems equally hideous and revolting. America is false to the past, false to the present, and solemnly binds herself to be false to the future. Standing with God and the crushed and bleeding slave on this occasion, I will, in the name of humanity which is outraged, in the name of liberty which is fettered, in the name of the constitution and the Bible which are disregarded and trampled upon, dare to call in question and to denounce, with all the emphasis I can command, everything that serves to perpetuate slavery the great sin and shame of America! I will not equivocate; I will not excuse; I will use the severest language I can command; and yet not one word shall escape me that any man, whose judgment is not blinded by prejudice, or who is not at heart a slaveholder, shall not confess to be right and just.

On a day made for acquiescence, Douglass cast a blinding light on the wrongs Negroes were suffering. He could not enjoy the independence celebration and take delight in his participation. Douglass did not ignore the suffering of his people, and would not allow America to. Douglass courageously and eloquently reminded America of the shame on its fabric of independence. Douglass aligned himself with his bondage brethren, although he no longer bore those chains.

Today's privileged African Americans must take the stance of Douglass. We must align ourselves with our less fortunate brothers and sisters in poor African American neighborhoods. We have to reinvest and take greater responsibility for our neighborhoods and community. The only way to accomplish this is by physically moving back to poor African American neighborhoods. Living there makes them our neighborhoods again. We will be steadfast in improving the conditions because they directly affect us. We now live there and our children will grow up there. Our futures and the African American community's must be joined again. Our lack of tolerance for the conditions in our community has driven us to flee. We decided, "I cannot live like that." Our return announces, **"We do not have to live like this."**

Lacking tolerance moved young African Americans of the 50's and 60's to resist Jim Crow. They knew a world different from their parents and grandparents. Their different perspective changed circumstances for the community. A transformation their elders believed impossible occurred. Today's privileged have a similar opportunity. We possess a perspective unlike the majority of our community living in poor neighborhoods. Physically returning will bring a transformation many in our community believe impossible. Impossible as a world where we no longer have to drink from separate water fountains or are refused service because of our race. We live that impossibility today.

An unwillingness to tolerate is our greatest asset as we return. The unwillingness to tolerate comes from seeing other communities thrive. We know that it can work. These tangible examples are the motivation for us to stop at nothing less than seeing the African American community flourish. Success in this migration is grounded in an unwillingness to tolerate. There will be forces inside and outside our community that will try to negotiate alternatives or bring about a settling outcome. There can be no compromise in the goal that we seek in this migration. The creation of thriving mixed-income African American neighborhoods will elevate our community to a place where future attempts at oppression will not be able to reach.

Past struggles were fights simply to be. To be recognized as human, to be recognized as equal citizens. Contemporary repressive forces have prevented us from stepping into the fullness of that being. Those forces have been successful in keeping our fight about surviving and not about thriving. A focus on thriving will destroy the present oppressive cycle replacing it with one of prosperity. An individual will easily choose education over selling drugs, despite their precarious financial situation. Thriving is grounded in long-term thinking that makes drug dealing impractical. Everyone knows there is no future in drug dealing. Young African Americans choose this trade because they see no future for themselves. Survival's short-term reasoning dictates entering the drug trade. Looking towards the horizon, not just a few steps ahead, produces perspective focused on a goal greater than today. One's tomorrows become of the utmost importance. An individual is willing to sacrifice today's instant gratification for the future. Realizing this is where the fullness of their being awaits.

OUR PEOPLE ARE NOT THE PROBLEM. OUR PEOPLE ARE NOT THE PROBLEM. OUR PEOPLE ARE NOT THE PROBLEM. OUR PEOPLE ARE NOT THE PROBLEM. OUR PEOPLE ARE NOT THE PROBLEM. OUR PEOPLE ARE NOT THE PROBLEM. OUR PEOPLE ARE NOT THE PROBLEM. OUR PEOPLE ARE NOT THE PROBLEM. OUR PEOPLE

ARE NOT THE PROBLEM. OUR PEOPLE ARE NOT THE PROBLEM. OUR PEOPLE ARE NOT THE PROBLEM. OUR PEOPLE ARE NOT THE PROBLEM. Privilege African Americans offer this notion as their rebuttal to returning. They argue return is futile because the current residents of poor African American neighborhoods are the biggest impediment to change. Ignorance, stubbornness, high propensity for violence, inertia, and low self-respect are the character traits that frustrate privileged African Americans. These behaviors are byproducts of the oppressive conditions set against the African American community. The fight can only begin with this recognition. The fight is not against our people. The fight is for our people and against oppression. **We must attack the conditions, not our people.**

The oppressive conditioning has a strong hold on our people. This conditioning is not contained within our neighborhoods. Even those no longer living in our poor neighborhoods can still suffer from the conditioning. African American rappers and professional athletes have achieved tremendous success and wealth. They have left behind those oppressive conditions in our poor neighborhoods. Yet, most still embody the conditioning from those neighborhoods. The drug and gang culture still reside with them. We frequently see professional athletes and rappers throwing up gang signs on television. A football player for my hometown Chicago Bears was recently indicted for drug trafficking. Underachievement in education is prevalent. Most rappers have not graduated from high school. Despite having full scholarships to top colleges and universities, most professional athletes do not have college degrees. Rappers and athletes make tons of money, but most end up financially distressed. The conditioning disables our people wherever they go. Without changing the conditioning our people are doomed inside and outside our neighborhoods.

Political capital is the greatest commodity missing within poor African American neighborhoods. The return of privileged African Americans will restore political capital to our neighborhoods. Political capital will tremendously impact the change we seek in our neighborhoods. Political capital is the tool communities utilize to secure government protection of their needs and interests. Constituencies of privileged individuals possess vast amounts of political capital. Highly productive individuals contribute a lot to our country. Their vital role elicits quick reactions from government entities. The political needs of a community with doctors, lawyers, professors, school principals, business owners, and other highly productive individuals will be satisfied.

Underprivileged constituencies in poor African American neighborhoods are ignored. Our country does not recognize their contributions as significant. Therefore their political needs are not addressed. The amalgamation of African American privileged and underprivileged in neighborhoods will stop the neglect of our underprivileged. Privileged African Americans' unwillingness to tolerate the conditions brings a voice to issues of our underprivileged that can no longer be ignored. Our privileged returning to live in poor African American neighborhoods provides the political capital needed for change.

Law enforcement leads the fight against crime in neighborhoods and communities. It is not the duty of poor African Americans to fight off gangs and drug dealers. Residents play an important role, but they should not be the primary opposition. The blame cast on residents in poor African American neighborhoods is misplaced. The war on drugs, gangs, and crime is not their battle to lose. They are not failing themselves. Law enforcement has failed them.

Law enforcement protection is the greatest asset bought with political capital. Accountability of law enforcement is a vital component of a thriving neighborhood. Quality of police protections is a direct reflection of the political capital a neighborhood possesses. I currently live in the Hyde Park neighborhood of Chicago. This neighborhood has the political capital my West Side neighborhood does not. Living in Hyde Park I see the lines of protection drawn by political capital. My first Memorial Day weekend living in this neighborhood a young woman was shot and killed on the beach near me. This was shocking, murders do not occur in Hyde Park. The reaction of the police department was very different from murders and shootings in my West Side neighborhood. Following that tragedy the increased police presence on the beach and in the neighborhood was palpable. Police vehicles drove on the beach at night clearing it of people. Police officers on bicycles patrol the area all throughout the night. There was a clear effort to restore the feeling of peace to the residents. Hyde Park has a constituency the city of Chicago must protect. Hyde Park is home to the University of Chicago. In addition, Northwestern graduate students and professors live in this neighborhood and many other highly productive individuals. If the city of Chicago does not protect this constituency it will lose the positive affects it brings. The political capital of Hyde

Park has bought the vehement protection of the Chicago Police Department.

The lines of protection are very clear in my city of Chicago. The many murders in this city are very concentrated in neighborhoods without political capital like my West Side neighborhood. A great dichotomy exists in my city. This city has neighborhoods that are more dangerous than warzones, and neighborhoods with little or no violence. If the violence in my city is so uncontrollable, how is it contained within specific neighborhoods? The answer is the lines of protection drawn by political capital. My city is a microcosm of America. The violence and drug culture in poor African American neighborhoods is contained and tolerated around our country. Law enforcement in poor African American neighborhoods currently show-up to arrest, but not to protect. Many 911 calls for help are not responded to or the response is too delayed for protection. Our migration will change this. The combination of political capital and unwillingness to tolerate the violence and drug culture will bring accountability to law enforcement in our neighborhoods. A neighborhood of individuals with political capital and individuals without political capital will receive the same protection as a neighborhood with only individuals with political capital. The traditional demarcation between the two groups is no longer possible. To protect those individuals of value you must protect the entire neighborhood. Local governments will have to ensure our neighborhoods are safe. The migration will place poor African American neighborhoods inside those lines of protection.

Political capital is also bought through the exercise of our collective voice. We cannot blame the first African American President or any politician that does not address our needs and interest if we do not demand it. Our collective voice facilitates the demand by shaping the political climate. No past President has been a champion for African American causes. The characterization of Abraham Lincoln and John F. Kennedy as such is false. The political climate of the time required placement of our community's issue atop their agenda. The efforts of abolitionists and world community scrutiny forced our sixteenth President to end slavery. The Civil Rights Movement pushed JFK and Lyndon Johnson towards African American equality. Kennedy felt those issues were distracting from the Cold War. Today gay rights and immigration are atop our President's agenda because the collective voice of those communities is deafening.

The African American community has become too quiet.
We raised our voice over the tragedy in Sanford, Florida.
We moved our President from taking the hands off approach,
declaring it a state issue. To using his executive power to
influence justice be done. A product of our migration will
be the rising of our collective voice. Desegregation split
our collective voice. United communities began to drown out
our community's cries. Reuniting, our cries will place our
needs and interests aside gay rights and immigration
issues. With the re-election of our President the
reemergence of our collective voice will be timely as ever.
Creating a political climate for the first African American
President to address the African American community's
issues is our opportunity, not his duty.

Returning privileged African Americans must open
businesses in our poor neighborhoods. We must out compete
the exploitive businesses. Creating businesses of higher
quality service and products will eliminate the economic
exploitation. Harnessing our community's spending power is
essential to creating thriving mixed-income neighborhoods.
Control of our spending power allows us to create an
internal economy. An internal economy assures self-
sustainability. Dollars circulating through our
neighborhoods provide local jobs. New employment

opportunities will reciprocate a strong local consumer base. A cycle of economic stability will develop. The jobs supplied by neighborhood businesses provide a livelihood for local employees. They in turn patronize neighborhood businesses, keeping them open for business. Creating economic opportunities within our neighborhoods is central to saving our community. It ensures our people have alternatives to selling drugs.

The migration's greatest achievement will be quality education in poor African American neighborhoods. Our schools are a direct reflection of our neighborhoods' condition. Transforming the neighborhood transforms our schools. Ignorance is the greatest weapon of oppression. Consequently, education is oppression's kryptonite. Thriving neighborhoods produce thriving schools. The increased tax base will provide our neighborhood schools with proper funding. Our political capital will hold educators accountable, from administrators to teachers. Thriving businesses, increased homeownership, and decreased crime together cultivate quality education. Quality education secures our community's future. Education more than money will sustain our people. Remember, "A fool and is money soon parts." However, "Education is the key to unlock the golden door of freedom." Also, "Education is a precondition to survival in America." The African American community has too long been denied quality education. This tool guarantees our equality more than any law. By creating thriving mixed-income neighborhoods we secure it for ourselves.

Privileged African Americans have not totally abandoned our community. Through charity some reach back and try to exact change. However, charity is not enough. Charity is a bandage on a womb that requires staples. A morning bus ride in my West Side neighborhood drove this point home for me. A young lady, no more than fifteen, boarded the bus with some other children. The bus driver said something to anger her. The young lady proceeded to curse out the bus driver and all of us passengers for our reactions. Her rage affected me the most. Hearing the language she was using was not unusual. However, the level and rapidity of her rage made me sit back and search for understanding. Rather than cast this young lady away as ignorant and unreachable. I took notice of the young lady's, and the children she boarded the bus with, clothing. Their clothing was dirty and wrinkled. It was the first day of public school in Chicago. I now knew where her hurt, disguised as rage, was coming from. I knew what it was like to not have new clothes for the start of the school year. My bathtub was once my Laundromat. My mother once used vouchers to shop at a thrift store for my school clothes. Both she and I knew what ridicule awaited at her public school, not just the first day, but everyday.

Most would extend charity to help this young lady. Simply buy her the clothes she needed for school. This solution covers up the problem it does not fix it. The young lady needs self-worth. Self-worth too often in the African American community comes from material possessions. We cannot create a utopia where no one suffers from want. We can create an African American community that provides the self-worth our children need. Our neighborhoods should possess institutions of affirmation. The primary institution of affirmation should be our public schools. A shopping spree would immediately, but temporarily soothe the young lady's hurt. A quality education would provide self-worth and change her focus from clothing to her future. Clothing will always become old and dirty, but a quality education is timeless. Self-worth should go deeper than the clothes on our back. African American neighborhoods are sparse with signs of self-worth. Our migration back will be the first sign we put up.

Thriving mixed-income African American neighborhoods is the purpose of our migration. Gentrification will threaten to push out low-income residents. There are methods to combat this negative externality of our return. We must put in place protections for low-income residents. A grandfather clause can protect homeowners fearing an increase in property tax. Tax rates will not rise on those properties until the owner changes. The improving conditions should benefit loyal homeowners the most. The neighborhood's tax base will increase from the taxes new homeowners pay. Low-income renters can be protected as well. Owners of rental property can make a commitment to accepting public housing residents. Rent control laws can further secure affordable housing in our neighborhoods. These suggestions are not exhaustive. They may not be the best solutions. These are merely options. We do not have to fear gentrification. Its negative effects can be prevented. Neighborhoods across our country are made up of different income levels. The suburb adjacent my West Side neighborhood has million dollar homes, middle-class homes, and affordable low-income rental and homeowner property. Gentrification's negative externalities have a racial undertone. Usually the migrating population is a different race than the current population. The racial disconnect aids in the economic removal of low-income residents. People do not sympathize as much with those who are different. Our migration is driven by sympathy for our community's underprivileged. **_The work of inclusion is our chosen duty._**

The Great Migration was the movement of my grandparents' generation from rural southern towns to northern industrial cities. This generation of migrators sought a better life in northern cities with more job opportunities and less racial oppression than the south. The Great Migration was very significant for our people. The migration put more distance between African Americans and our past of subjugation. Future generations would not know the anguish of living on the land of tremendous suffering for our ancestors. This book calls for a greater migration than the 1900's. Throughout our turbulent history in this country our community has always been a refuge. We were the safest in our community, if nowhere else. Today African American life is most threatened within our community. Our migration has higher stakes than our grandparents' migration. The Great Migration was all about geography. The geographical shift bettered our community's future. Our migration has nothing to do with geography. Poor African American neighborhoods are all around this country: north, south, east, and west. The Great Migration was to improve the future. Our migration is a fight to keep a future possible.

Our community is dying! Despite the many gains of the past African American achievement is declining. Doors of opportunities are being closed and locked forever. African American youth are more likely to experience gang violence, drug addiction, drug selling, teen pregnancy, high school failure, illiteracy, and/or HIV/AIDS rather than college graduation, financial security, and/or marriage. The African American community has no future if this remains the reality of our children. Our migration changes this reality and restores our community's future.

"If you dare to struggle, you dare to win."

The Inalienable Choice

The Declaration of Independence declares "life, liberty, and the pursuit of happiness" as inalienable rights endowed to all human beings. The recognition of equality in all men is a powerful element of the document. However, the document's essence was not the inalienable rights but protection of those rights. Human beings live and breathe with an inalienable choice which guards against tyranny. The Declaration of Independence is the manifestation of this inalienable choice. **Revolution is our inalienable choice.** Humanity's greatest weapon is revolution. Revolution dwells within the individual and cannot be removed. The individual defines and shapes revolution. The individual determines the start and finish line of revolution. Revolution is an individual's sovereignty to change their now.

The migration is not only about privileged African Americans returning to our poor neighborhoods. The battle for mixed-income African American neighborhoods is twofold. Underprivileged African Americans must exercise their inalienable choice. They must choose revolution. There is a deep yearning within our underprivileged. They are not content with life's despair. They are not blind to the oppressive forces beating upon them. Still, they see no way of changing their circumstances. A former high school classmate expressed this sentiment to me. He spoke about the many regrets he carried. Education was the biggest. He now realized the importance of an education. He wants so badly another chance at getting an education. Despite his strong desire, an intense doubt walked with him. He believed his past choices made it impossible for him to gain an education. He was defeated. Many African American underprivileged, like my high school classmate, are not aware of their inalienable choice. My former classmate is in his mid-twenties. "How long do you expect to live", I asked him? I reminded him that he had more than double the lifetime he has already lived ahead of him. If he dedicated himself wholeheartedly to obtaining an education, his life's trajectory can change in five years. "Your past choices have made getting an education harder, but not impossible." Underprivileged African Americans' past choices have made their road to prosperity longer, but it is not a dead end. Revolution preserves prosperity for the individual who is willing to sacrifice for it.

Revolution is not always a grandiose display or fight for transformation. You can stage a personal revolution that is confined to your life. My mother started a revolution after seeing her faults as a parent with her oldest child. She vowed to not lose another child to the inner city streets. She sacrificed to put her remaining children in private school for the majority of their education. When financial struggles forced her to enroll the two older children into public high schools her revolution intensified. She became deeply involved as a parent. Making sure the principal and teachers knew her children were there to be taught. Through her efforts she has seen her two older children become middle class, homeowners, and dedicated husbands and fathers. She has seen her youngest child graduate from the top liberal arts college in the nation, and soon from a top tier law school. Her revolution has impacted all the generations to follow her. Her grandchildren have not experienced the struggles her children and she endured. Revolution can blaze a trail for the world or for just you and your family. An individual's decision to take their life back from life's autopilot is the start point of revolution.

Our migration will challenge underprivileged African Americans to be more accountable for their lives. As conditions improve the present valid excuses will disappear. There will be resistance from some living in poor African American neighborhoods. We are not a perfect race. Some will never embrace accountability. There are unchangeable underachievers among us. No matter the conditions these people will not work for better. Those who benefit from the drug trade will mount the greatest opposition. We know that if the gangbangers and drug dealers were to stop tomorrow America has nothing to offer them. "How will we survive", they will ask? "Stand with us and demand America provide you with an option other than dying", we reply. ***Chose revolution!*** Some have become content with the conditions. They do not want to see anything change. "Ignorance is bliss." This minority of people will have to create a community of underachievers outside of the African American community. There is no place for them in our thriving mixed-income neighborhoods. Our community must move ahead without them.

Revolution is not popular because it inevitably involves suffering. The price of revolution is some degree of suffering. Certainty of victory does not alleviate the uneasiness of this requirement. Human nature is to avoid or prevent hurt. The biblical example is Jesus in the Garden of Gethsemane asking, "Let this cup pass from me." No one was more certain of victory than Jesus. Yet, he asked for relief. Privileged and underprivileged African Americans have different fears about the migration. Plato's "Allegory

of the Cave" illustrates underprivileged African Americans'
fears.

And now, I said, let me show in a figure how far
our nature is enlightened or unenlightened: --
Behold! Human beings living in a underground
cave, which has a mouth open towards the light
and reaching all along the cave; here they have
been from their childhood, and have their legs
and necks chained so that they cannot move, and
can only see before them, being prevented by the
chains from turning round their heads. Above and
behind them a fire is blazing at a distance, and
between the fire and the prisoners there is a
raised way; and you will see, if you look, a low
wall built along the way, like the screen which
marionette players have in front of them, over
which they show the puppets.

To them, I said, the truth would be literally
nothing but the shadows of the images.

And now look again, and see what will naturally
follow if the prisoners are released and
disabused of their error. At first, when any of
them is liberated and compelled suddenly to stand
up and turn his neck round and walk and look
towards the light, he will suffer sharp pains;
the glare will distress him, and he will be
unable to see the realities of which in his
former state he had seen the shadows; and then
conceive some one saying to him, that what he saw
before was an illusion, but that now, when he is
approaching nearer to being and his eye is turned
towards more real existence, he has a clearer
vision, -what will be his reply? And you may
further imagine that his instructor is pointing
to the objects as they pass and requiring him to
name them, -will he not be perplexed? Will he not
fancy that the shadows which he formerly saw are
truer than the objects which are now shown to
him?

And suppose once more, that he is reluctantly
dragged up a steep and rugged ascent, and held
fast until he 's forced into the presence of the

> sun himself, is he not likely to be pained and
> irritated? When he approaches the light his eyes
> will be dazzled, and he will not be able to see
> anything at all of what are now called realities.

Plato's allegory demonstrates the painful process of stepping into a new reality. Freedom can be scarier than remaining imprisoned. It is easy to blame the chains. Removal of the chains creates responsibility for your own reality. The light has many possibilities for shaping reality. No such burdens exist inside the cave. However, enlightenment's touch creates internal conflict. The reality of the cave carries a greater burden. The vexing knowledge of another reality resides inside the cave with you now. Your reality is altered by the mere knowledge of the light. The unsettling nature of enlightenment causes many to avoid its touch.

Mixed-income African American neighborhoods will be a new reality for underprivileged African Americans. These neighborhoods will bring new possibilities akin to the light in the cave. The opportunities for change will be within the grasp of our underprivileged, unlike before. This new reality converts oppression from a chain into a choice. The choice of oppression is more unbearable than to wear its chain. The migration's success will alter reality for all underprivileged African Americans. Taking no part

will not preserve anyone's reality. The migration has a
certainty of suffering for underprivileged African
Americans. Action or inaction causes discomfort.
Capitalizing from the new opportunities requires the gritty
work of progress. Continued cave dwelling will cause an
agony greater than past inertia. Underprivileged African
Americans fears the migration because it will inevitably
unsettle their reality.

Dr. King's "I've Been To The Mountaintop" speech is
instructive on privileged African Americans reservations.
His usage of the parable of the Good Samaritan from the
Bible best illustrates. The parable is about a man who was
beaten and left on the side of a road in the town of
Jericho. Two men passed by the man without helping him. The
Good Samaritan stopped to give aid to the fallen man. Dr.
King inquires as to why the two men passed by while the
Samaritan stopped. The answer, he says, lies in the
internal question those men asked. "If I stop to help this
man what will happen to me?" Privileged African Americans
will pose this same question in regard to the migration.
Many of us have gained so much in life. It will be
difficult to risk those achievements for this migration.
Thoughts of loss will push many to pass by like the men on

that road to Jericho. However, Dr. King called on those not in need to sacrifice for those in need.

> [W]hen we have our march, you need to be there. If it means leaving work, if it means leaving school -- be there. Be concerned about your brother. You may not be on strike. But either we go up together, or we go down together.

> **Let us develop a kind of dangerous unselfishness**...

> And so the first question that the priest asked -- the first question that the Levite asked was, "If I stop to help this man, what will happen to me?" But then the Good Samaritan came by. And he reversed the question: "If I do not stop to help this man, what will happen to him?"

> That's the question before you tonight. Not, "If I stop to help the sanitation workers, what will happen to my job. Not, "If I stop to help the sanitation workers what will happen to all of the hours that I usually spend in my office every day and every week as a pastor?" The question is not, "If I stop to help this man in need, what will happen to me?" The question is, "If I do not stop to help the sanitation workers, what will happen to them?" That's the question.

The consideration over whether to join the migration should focus on what happens to the African American community if we do not return. The loss of our community will be far more devastating than any material, professional, or social loss we may encounter.

Our migration is revolution. As individuals we may encounter tragedy. Resolve will be our most effective weapon. We cannot let hurt, intimidation, or fear deter us at any point. **_We have to be driven with a fearless idealism_**. We cannot stop short of victory. Victory may take a lifetime. "Remember, don't quit until you either win or you die." A revolutionary who is not willing to put it all on the line is defeated before they start. The nature of opposition to revolution is to test its limits. Therefore, a revolutionary must not have any. We return with untiring determination to eradicate the oppressive conditions destroying our neighborhoods. We accept in full the burdens revolution requires. We will not stop until the inheritance of the African American community is secured for future generations. These are our limits.

All American historical figures we hold in high esteem desired and dedicated themselves to shaping their now. Our generation must not be afraid to do the same. We move ahead with reverence for the past. Nevertheless, we must not be afraid to alter the works of yesterday's revolutionaries to address the needs of today. We have to shape our now. We must trust our motives, and believe in the outcome we seek. Changing the conditions may not save many in the present. It will lay the foundation for future generations to obtain the American dream. We must exercise our inalienable choice. We must choose revolution, and start moving.

Seeing Is Believing

We must not underestimate the impact the mere presence of privileged African Americans can have in our poor neighborhoods. Filling the vacuum of role models is the least we will do. The daily sight of privileged African Americans will be powerful. It will inspire our youth to imagine new dreams. I experienced the start of those new imaginings when I moved back to the West Side of Chicago. I could afford to live elsewhere but decided to be an example of different possibilities for youth in my neighborhood. I did not have to interact with them. I simply had to be seen. One day my friend overheard two young men on the corner speaking about me. The first young man mocked my business attire saying, "Look what he's wearing." The second young man responded, "But look at what he's driving." There is a message in the sheer presence of privileged African Americans. A new thought process develops inside African American youth about how to achieve the lifestyles they desire. Without saying a word I sparked new thought in those young men. Our youth's thinking will change when the sight of African American professionals counteracts the sight of drug dealers in their neighborhoods. Getting African American youth to question their choices, and evaluate alternatives is well worth the return.

African American athletes and entertainers are relieved of their duty as default role models to our youth. The qualifications for being a role model go well beyond an individual's bank account. Striving to set an example in every aspect of your life is the defining quality of a role model. These surrogate role models are rife with hypocrisy. The lifestyles led by most athletes and entertainers contradict a message of growth. The message conveyed by their lifestyle is that money immunizes you from maturity, morality, abiding by the law, and respect for others. A message of self-respect and value of education is confusing from a person who lacks an education and is on the Internet "making it rain" in strip clubs. Being a role model is a great responsibility. Few choose to burden themselves with it. Our entertainers and athletes have had this burden unfairly placed upon them. The inspiration and guidance of African American youth should not be imposed upon these individuals. Only those willing to accept the responsibility should carry the duty of role model.

In an interview Bill Cosby said he could not stop being an activist in his elderly years because young black men are dying. I was ashamed of my generation after hearing this. Bill Cosby and our elders should be able to pass the baton of justice and progress to us. They should rest assured we will carry it farther into the future. However, they find themselves still on the front lines because too many of our generation have not answered the call. It is our time to take the front lines. It is time to conquer our generation's momentary impossibility. From the sidelines our elders will watch with pride and joy at the sight of our giants, like their giants, being defeated.

We must not encourage the African American community to accept second-class assistance from the United States government. Many of today's role models call on our community to accept scraps to disprove lethargy. Comparing our community's yearnings to those of blacks in third world countries. How little they seek versus how much we demand. Not recognizing their country's few resources dictates those yearnings. The United States spends billions annually supporting the infrastructure of other countries. Our nation offers first-class aid to foreigners. As American citizens why should our community accept less than first-class assistance as well? Those fortunate young women of Oprah Winfrey's South Africa boarding school would find it difficult returning to their former classrooms in shacks. Their experience would move them to no longer accept a

shack as a classroom. They would demand better because they
have known better. A role model's purpose is to evoke
change in the demands of those you inspire. Change in what
they demand from themselves, their community, and their
country. The African American community's demands are on
par with what the United States can deliver, and has
delivered to others. As role models we must join in their
demands, not criticize them.

Our migration is not self-segregation. Desegregation
was about the destruction of African American second-class
citizenship not diversity. New York City is the exemplar of
racial diversity in our country. The Big apple is an
aberration. Majority of our country still consist of
homogeneous neighborhoods. The idea that desegregation was
about community diversity and not social and legal equality
is bogus. America's integration has been imbalanced from
its inception. American integration is African Americans
moving to homogenous Caucasian neighborhoods. This
imbalanced integration furthers white supremacy. It keeps
prosperity confined within Caucasian spheres. Thriving
mixed-income African American neighborhoods will create a
balanced integration. It will spread prosperity beyond
Caucasian spheres. Our neighborhoods are ideal for
integration. We will not lock other races out of our

neighborhoods. We do not have a history of discrimination. African Americans do not live with fear of other races. Therefore we are able to live next to other races peacefully. Mixed-income African American neighborhoods will create greater equality in America.

Detractors of my book will come from inside and outside the African American community. They will refute all my arguments as untrue or hyperbole. Many will place blame solely on the shoulders of the African American underprivileged. Denials of today's residual effects from slavery and the systematic oppression of our community will be abundant. Privileged African Americans will repudiate the idea their choosing to live in Caucasian neighborhoods furthers our community's inferiority. Some will call my examples of Blackness under attack exaggeration and isolated incidents. The ideas in this book will generate strong emotion. The emotional responses are generated by human nature to not disturb the order of the day. Even if the order of the day is oppression of others. Dr. King and the Freedom Riders experienced similar reactions. Few in the African American community thought it prudent to face the dangers of challenging segregation in interstate travel. From a Birmingham jail cell Dr. King expressed to his detractors why justice and equality is never untimely.

I do not mind dissent. I expect it. I accept it. To disagree and offer no alternative is unacceptable. Something must be done. **What is your solution?**

There has always been an effort to ignore the plight of African Americans in our country. I have found it impossible. I initially planned to have a personal migration back to my Chicago neighborhood. I would exact whatever change I could on my own. However, GOD instructed me to write this invitation to privileged African Americans. Join me in Chicago, or migrate back to Detroit, Oakland, Baltimore, D.C., New York City, New Orleans, St. Louis, Houston, Los Angeles or Newark. Wherever you find African American neighborhoods in need of change, ignite revolution. You may find yourself alone wherever you decide to migrate. Many will not initially partake in this migration. Do not underestimate the impact one dedicated individual can have on a neighborhood, a community, this world. Be that shining example, and with your success, watch the tide turn and many migrate.

History told my generation about the ills of segregation and the South. The freedoms we enjoy make Jim Crow inconceivable for us. We cannot imagine living in a world of such subjugation. Those who fought before us did not leave us a perfect world, but a better one. We must reciprocate this change for the next generation. Fifty years from now our reality should be an unimaginable piece of history for African American youth. Our grandchildren should ask us, "What was it like to live under those circumstances?" The same question we had to ask of our grandparents. Future generations should read about the violence, gangs, and drugs with wide eyes. Their awe will be coupled with gratitude because they live a better reality. Join the migration.

"Tonight, my friends I find, in being black, a thing of beauty: a joy; a strength; a secret cup of gladness; a native land in neither time nor place, a native land in every Negro face! Be loyal to yourselves: your skin; your hair; your lips, your southern speech, your laughing kindness are Negro Kingdoms, vast as any other! Accept in full the sweetness of your blackness, not wishing to be red, nor white, nor yellow: nor any race, or face, but this. Farewell, my deep Africanic brothers, be brave, keep freedom in the family..."

www.ingramcontent.com/pod-product-compliance
Lightning Source LLC
Chambersburg PA
CBHW081544040426
42448CB00015B/3220